# ENCHANTED CIRCLES

# ENCHANTED CIRCLES

Elizabeth Jane Lloyd

*To all the circles of the turning year*

Conran Octopus

First published in 1990 by
**Conran Octopus Limited**
37 Shelton Street, London WC2H 9HN

PROJECT EDITOR    *Polly Powell*
ART EDITOR    *Prue Bucknall*

TEXT    *Lorraine Dickey*
COPY EDITOR    *Debora Robertson*
EDITORIAL ASSISTANTS    *Christine Rickerby and Helen Ridge*
PICTURE RESEARCHER    *Kathy Lockley*
PRODUCTION    *Bruce Carter*
SPECIAL PHOTOGRAPHY    *Jan Baldwin, Jacqui Hurst and David Phelps*
ILLUSTRATOR    *Vanessa Luff*
ILLUSTRATIONS ON PAGES 11, 37, 61 AND 95    *Elizabeth Jane Lloyd*
STYLIST    *Hilary Robertson*

British Library Cataloguing in Publication Data
Lloyd, Elizabeth Jane
Enchanted circles: the art of making wreaths,
garlands and decorative rings.
1. Handicrafts
I. Title
745.92

ISBN 1 85029 271 X

Typeset by Litho Link Limited, Welshpool, Powys, Wales
Printed and bound in Hong Kong

CAPTIONS TO ILLUSTRATIONS ON PAGES 1-3
PAGE 1: *A simple wired wreath of feathers, painted eggs and decorative*
*birds (for technique, see pages 30-31 and 122-125).*
PAGE 2: *Wired wreath of herbs and green chillis (for technique, see pages 42-3).*
PAGE 3: *A collage of pebbles and feathers gleaned from a country walk.*

# CONTENTS

# INTRODUCTION

Throughout the world, in every culture, circles and rings have had a mythical potency for mankind since the earliest times. The spherical shapes of the sun, moon and earth and the natural cycle of the seasons formed the bases of many early rites and religions. As it was from these 'circles' that life itself derived, early peoples sought out other occurrences of the magical shape in nature, as well as creating representations of it for themselves.

The circle is used as a symbol to signify love, protection, friendship, rebirth, and even life itself. From early Paganism the circle – whether in the form of ritual dances or symbolic decorations – has formed an important part of secular and religious ceremonies for many centuries.

Dance has always been one way in which Man defined and confirmed a sense of community. Mediterranean, African and native American cultures all developed highly ritualistic dances, frequently as an expression of joy, for example to celebrate a marriage, but also as an affirmation of power, as in the widespread tradition of communal dancing. Such dances involve the participants in forming a circle which is at once joyful, protective and re-enforcing.

In North America, native tribes used circles as empowering and protective symbols. Round headdresses and tepees arranged in circles are two examples, but perhaps the most fascinating manifestation of this kind of symbolism is the tradition of sand painting. In some tribes, this solemn ritual would be carried out by a young warrior who would use his foot to draw a circle around himself.

The circle, or the wheel of life and death, is used in many forms of Islamic, Hindu and Buddhist decoration. Some significant examples of the use of the circle are found in the Tibetan mandala used in meditation.

In many societies the circle represents equality and democracy. African tribal meetings were traditionally held with all of the senior members of the tribe sitting in a large circle so that each person could give his opinion. The English king, Arthur, created a round table for his knights so that they would all appear to be equal. Even today, the European Community's symbol of unity is a circle of golden stars, one for each of the member states, on a plain blue background.

For many people all over the world the exchange of rings marks one of life's most significant rituals – marriage. The never-ending circle of a fine gold band signifies eternity and fidelity, it blesses the new phase of the wearer's life and draws upon the protective symbolism of the circle.

Since the earliest times, the circle has represented spiritual protection. Like the moat around a castle, it is not just the circle itself that is important, it is the still, tranquil, safe place it creates in its centre. For this reason it is the most important shape in many religions and cultures and is drawn upon in meditation and prayer because it symbolizes hope and perpetual renewal.

Wreath making is one of the most ancient of crafts and one which is inextricably entwined with Man's historic desire to recreate nature's own circles. Traditionally made from plants – as organic material formed into a circle was seen as a way of linking the maker and the wearer to everlasting life – such ancient symbols join us to our past and confirm our place in a centuries' old tradition.

In ancient Greece, wreaths of laurel, oak and olive leaves were bestowed upon the winners of athletic or poetic competitions as well as anyone of importance. The Romans absorbed this tradition and honoured victorious generals with laurel wreaths – indeed, even today it is quite common for the highest military honours to represent oak or laurel leaves in their design. Eventually, wreaths made from foliage were replaced by

those made of gold, for example when Napoleon crowned himself Emperor of France in 1804, he did so with a gleaming crown of golden laurel leaves.

The tradition of wreath making and wearing is not exclusive to great emperors and ancient poets. All over the world, people make garlands and circles for seasonal festivals, special family celebrations and simply to decorate their homes throughout the year. This craft has grown up independently in many different countries as far apart as India and Poland. The range of materials is immense, from simple garlands of spring flowers made almost everywhere, to elaborate woven hangings of brilliantly coloured yarn in Mexico or delicate circles of hand-painted eggs in Eastern Europe.

However diverse the materials, the festivals and celebrations are often the same – birth, weddings, Christmas, New Year, Easter or harvest. For example, throughout Europe the ancient tradition of brides wearing a circlet of flowers and her young attendants carrying hoops of blossoms is enjoying renewed popularity. In many cultures, floral headdresses are worn by both bride and groom, each one simultaneously representing a halo, crown and wreath. Haloes emphasize the purity and virtue of the pair; crowns celebrate their union; and wreaths mark the passing of the first stage of their lives.

In Greece, even today, the whole family participates in making the wedding bread, a circular centre-piece decorated with cut-out symbols of

good fortune and well-being.

As well as celebration, wreaths have traditionally had a practical purpose. Circles made of flowers, grasses and crops such as corn and barley were a good way of drying and preserving seeds for the next season. In many rural areas, elaborate harvest-time rituals were associated with the weaving of these circles. They were made from the last sheaf to be harvested not just to preserve the seed, but also, it was believed, to preserve the spirit of the earth until the following year.

Wreaths, circles and garlands have a noble and fascinating history and when you begin to make your own you will be entering into a special centuries' old tradition.

There are a few better ways of capturing a special moment than this – use your imagination, draw on your immediate surroundings for inspiration and, as well as being decorative, your wreaths will become unique and lasting keepsakes to treasure.

CAPTIONS TO ILLUSTRATIONS ON PAGES 6 AND 7.
TOP ROW, FROM LEFT TO RIGHT:
*False colour image of the sun; earth, photographed from the Apollo 17 spacecraft in 1972; false colour image of a diatom; cross-section through the trunk of an oak tree; spider's web; waves produced by a droplet of water.*
CENTRE ROW: *Buddhist tanka painting; Persian painting of a flight through the celestial spheres; the north rose window of Notre Dame, Paris; Yin-yang symbol; sixteenth-century astrological chart; clock face at Hampton Court Palace.*
BOTTOM ROW: *Leonardo da Vinci's representation of Man's proportions; French village settlement; Syrian folk-dancers; wooden cartwheel; Portuguese windmill; compact disc.*

# SPRING

*Love is a circle that doth restless move*
*In the same sweet eternity of love*
LOVE WHAT IT IS
ROBERT HERRICK

# 'WELL COME' TO THE WORLD

Down the centuries, childbirth has been surrounded by ritual and magic – it was such a hazardous affair, that the joy of creation was always tainted by the fear of death. In ancient Greece, wreaths were attached to the door of a home to announce and bless a baby's safe passage into the world – olive leaves signified a boy, and a wool band or ribbon, a girl.

In many parts of Britain, friends and relatives traditionally gave the newborn baby presents of salt, eggs, bread and matches – salt for a healthy body and healthy mind; eggs for fertility and immortality; bread to ensure all the necessities of life; and matches to signify the path of light from the mortal world to heaven.

The exact moment of a child's birth is considered by many to play a part in his or her destiny. In 3000BC, Babylonian priests observed the patterns of the sun, moon and planets, believing that the cycles of movement might govern the seemingly random course of events on earth. In many cultures, wealthy parents would engage an astrologer to be present at the birth of their child so that, knowing the exact time, date and location of the baby's birth, they could predict the child's path through life accurately. Even today, many people still believe that a person's birth sign influences their character.

An unusual gift for a newborn baby would be a watercolour circle like the one shown opposite. If you do not feel confident enough to paint one yourself, you could make a unique collage using pictures of the baby's family, clippings from newspapers, labels and small toys – in fact, anything that reflects the world into which the baby is born.

The moment of birth is a portentous time, and good luck gifts, such as this circle of a baby's footprints, are still an essential part of a child's welcome to the world. If you want to make this kind of keepsake, remember to use a water-based paint.

Like an ancient baptism, a circle or ring puts the newborn child into the circular framework of life and is a perfect symbol of family renewal.

RIGHT: *Water-based paint is used to make this circle of tiny footprints.*

OPPOSITE: *An astrological circle in watercolours would make a special gift for new parents.*

WELCOME TO THE WORLD . 1989 . 9.45 16th Pm 12th HUMPHREY . W . WOOD

# VALENTINE CIRCLES

ABOVE: *Stiff card forms the base for this amusing circle of plastic cherubs and lace ribbons — a suitable gift for a child.*
OPPOSITE: *Shiny red satin hearts are sewn into a ring and studded with pearls.*

ince the eighteenth century, it has been the custom to exchange anonymous love-tokens on 14 February. Over the centuries, many amusing 'mating' games developed: *'It is a ceremony, never omitted among the Vulgar'*, one eighteenth-century record states when referring to these traditional games. It continues *'The names of a select number of one sex are by an equal number of the other put into some vessel; and after that everyone draws a name, which for the present is called their Valentine, and is also look'd upon as a good omen of their being man and wife afterwards'.*

The element of chance is still alive today in the tradition that the first member of the opposite sex seen on the morning of 14 February is supposed to be your Valentine.

A Valentine circle is a particularly romantic gift to give to someone

ABOVE: *A simple wired ring of miniature
roses and rue. For technique,
see pages 122-125.*

OPPOSITE: '*A circular bowl containing dampened
Oasis, overflowing with violets and
miniature roses.*

close. In common with other traditional love tokens, such as Welsh love spoons or Victorian cut-paper greetings, the more elaborate and labour-intensive the offering, the more sincere the affection is supposed to be.

For your Valentine circle, you could, as one alternative, forget the turbulent emotions associated with this time of year and make a light-hearted ring like some of the ones shown here. The

first (see page 14), is made from small, synthetic cherubs and lace. To make this type of wreath you will need to cut a piece of stiff card into a circle with a diameter of approximately 9in (23cm). Use a strong, bonding glue to attach lace ribbons and love tokens of your choice. The second (see page 15), is a glamorous concoction of red satin hearts and tiny fake pearls that have been sewn together. Alterna-

tively, you could choose flowers and decorations for their associations and meanings (see page 26), such as tulips which symbolize the heart burning like a flame. Or, what could be more romantic than a circle made of fresh or dried lavender, roses, jonquil, and red and blue salvia, meaning respectively, devotion, love, 'I desire a return of affection', 'I think of you' and 'forever mine'?

# SPRING FLOWERS

ABOVE: *Pressed pansies are stuck onto a simple*
*card base with strong glue.*
OPPOSITE: *White chrysanthemum heads are*
*attached to a polystyrene base with U-shaped pins.*

The bringing in of the May was originally a magical rite celebrated to ensure the revival of nature in spring. The sight of the first buds and the sun rising higher in the sky were the visible signs that the enchantment was working.

Phillip Stubbes, the English Puritan, was sure that during the traditional spring festivities there was *'a great Lord present ... namely, Sathan, prince of hel.'* Pagans, however, would have argued that it was not Satan who was present, but the spirit of the earth renewing itself and the tree spirits hailing rejuvenation and the arrival of a fertile new season.

The maypole was frequently made of hawthorn, a symbol of joy at the return of spring, and hawthorn leaves were often woven into a wreath for the representative of the 'spirit of the woods' to wear.

The newly-cut tree used for the pole was thought to bring with it the spirit of vegetation. The first flower of spring and the fair young girl chosen to be May Queen were both thought to be signs of the spirit's presence. The spirit of vegetation was also the bringer of the harvest, so when you make a ring of fresh spring flowers, you are not only celebrating spring but completing the circle as a blessing for the future harvest.

In Lincolnshire, England, the town of Spalding has a special way of celebrating the arrival of spring. Each year the first flowers are plucked to

ABOVE: *Small bunches of delicate flowers are threaded together on wire. For technique, see pages 122-125.*

OPPOSITE: *The wired flowers, including heather, pansies and grape hyacinths, are tied together to make a wreath.*

promote stronger bulbs for the next year. The flowerheads are then used to decorate floats used in an annual procession through the town. On a smaller scale, you could use the same principle to make an attractive table centre using flower heads, attached to a 24in (60cm) circle of polystyrene with U-shaped pins (see page 19).

Although these different kinds of spring celebrations, especially maypole decoration, are most common in northern parts of Europe, some form of spring festival is held in most countries throughout the world.

In the Kanagra district of India, young girls celebrated the fair of Rali (Rali is a small clay image of the god of vegetation). Each day for ten days, the girls took baskets of grass and flowers to an appointed place where they threw them onto a pile. At the end of the ten days, when the pile was quite high, the images of the vegetation gods were ceremonially placed on top. After feasting – and in a spirit of high emotion – the images were thrown into the river and wept over as though it were a funeral. In one sense it was: the object of this rite was to

secure a good husband, so in the Rali ceremony the girls are really marking the passing of their girlhood and the advent of a new stage in their lives.

Spring is traditionally the time for lovers, so take advantage of the abundance of new, beatifully scented spring flowers and make a romantic circle of your own. Or you could make a simple daisy chain, one of the earliest and most evocative celebrations of spring. Whatever you choose to do, you will be drawing on one of the most ancient and potent symbols of renewal and fertility.

Against May, Whitsonday, or other time, all
the yung men and maides, olde men and
wives, run gadding over night to the woods,
groves, hils, and mountains, where they
spend all the night in pleasant pastimes; and
in the morning they return, bringing with
them birch and branches of trees, to dock
their assemblies withall . . . But the chiefest
jewel they bring from thence is their May-pole
. . . which is covered all over with floures and
hearbs . . . then fall they to daunce about it,
like as the heathen people did at the
dedication of the idols.

PHILLIP STUBBES, 1583

ABOVE: *Snowdrops are threaded into a vine base.*
*For technique, see pages 122-125.*
RIGHT: *Snowdrops and grape hyacinths are*
*typical components of a spring circle.*

OPPOSITE: A *similar vine base is enlivened with*
*azaleas and* Iris reticulata.

# THE LANGUAGE OF FLOWERS

| | | | | | |
|---|---|---|---|---|---|
| ACACIA | *secret love* | HEARTSEASE | *remembrance* | ORANGE BLOSSOM | *purity, loveliness* |
| ALMOND BLOSSOM | *sweetness, hope* | HIBISCUS | *delicate beauty* | | |
| AMARANTH | *immortality* | HOLLY | *hope, divinity* | PANSIES | *love, 'thinking of you'* |
| AMARYLLIS | *pride, splendid beauty* | HONESTY | *wealth* | PEACH BLOSSOM | *long life* |
| ANEMONE | *withered hopes, foresaken* | HONEYSUCKLE | *devotion* | PEONY | *bashfulness* |
| APPLE BLOSSOM | *preference* | HYACINTH | *loveliness, constancy* | PERIWINKLE (BLUE) | *early friendship* |
| | | | | PERIWINKLE (WHITE) | *the pleasures of memory* |
| BELL FLOWER (WHITE) | *gratitude* | IVY | *eternity, fidelity* | PINKS | *love* |
| BLUEBELL | *constancy* | | | POINSETTIA | *fertility, eternity* |
| BROOM | *humility* | JASMINE (WHITE) | *amiability* | POPPY (RED) | *consolation* |
| BUTTERCUP | *childhood* | JASMINE (YELLOW) | *elegance, happiness* | | |
| | | JONQUIL | *'I desire a return of affection'* | ROSE (RED) | *love* |
| CAMELLIA | *excellence* | | | ROSE (YELLOW) | *jealousy* |
| CARNATION | *first love* | LAUREL | *triumph, eternity* | ROSEBUD | *pure and lovely* |
| CHRYSANTHEMUM (RED) | *'I love you'* | LAVENDER | *devotion, virtue* | | |
| CLEMATIS | *mental beauty, purity* | LILAC (PURPLE) | *first emotions* | SALVIA (BLUE) | *'forever mine'* |
| | | LILAC (WHITE) | *youthful innocence* | SALVIA (RED) | *'I think of you'* |
| DAFFODIL | *deceitful hopes* | LILY (WHITE) | *purity* | SNOWDROP | *hope, consolation* |
| DAISY | *innocence* | LILY (YELLOW) | *falsehood, gaiety* | STOCK | *lasting beauty* |
| DIANTHUS | *divine love* | LILY-OF-THE-VALLEY | *return of happiness* | SUNFLOWER | *haughtiness, false riches* |
| | | | | SWEET WILLIAM | *gallantry* |
| EVERGREEN | *life everlasting* | MAGNOLIA | *grief, pride, power* | | |
| EVERLASTING FLOWER | *unfading memory* | MARIGOLD | *joy* | TULIP (RED) | *declaration of love* |
| | | MICHAELMAS DAISY | *farewell* | TULIP (YELLOW) | *hopeless love* |
| FORGET-ME-NOT | *fidelity, true love* | MISTLETOE | *love* | | |
| | | | | VIOLET | *humility* |
| GARDENIA | *femininity* | NASTURTIUM | *patriotism* | | |
| GLADIOLUS | *incarnation* | | | WALLFLOWER | *fidelity in adversity* |
| | | OAK | *forgiveness, eternity* | | |
| HAWTHORN BLOSSOM | *hope* | OLIVE BRANCH | *peace* | ZINNIA | *'thinking of absent friends'* |

OPPOSITE: A *vine-based spring flower wreath including different varieties of*
*daffodils, tulips, rue, rosemary, catkins, lichen, cow parsley,* Viburnum
opulus *and variegated greenery.*

# DECORATED EGGS

ABOVE: *An easy-to-make table-centre
of loosely grouped helebores and
delicately coloured pink and
green pullet eggs.*

OPPOSITE: *Various types of decorated eggs,
some of which have had medium-gauge
wire threaded through their 'blow'
holes to form a circle.*

The return of spring has been celebrated since ancient times as the true beginning of a new year. Long before the advent of the holiest time in the Christian calendar, Easter, pagans held spring ceremonies that drew upon images of sacrifice and rebirth. Eggs have always been a very potent symbol of creation and regeneration, so it is hardly surprising that they have always been closely associated with these festivals.

Eggs play an important part in historic Egyptian and Chinese imagery, and the new year feast in Persia was known as the Feast of the Red Egg; red is the colour of blood, love and royalty and the red egg is a worldwide symbol of the resurrection.

Decorated eggs also have a illustrious past. The oldest existing one dates from AD4 and was found in a Roman sarcophagus in Germany.

The making of egg and feather circles is a craft practised in many countries and cultures to symbolize new birth. The eggs can be decorated using a variety of techniques, from dyeing and scraping to poster paints and felt-tip pens. Children, in particular, enjoy egg decorating and can develop all kinds of new techniques on their own. If they do not wish to make a circle with their eggs, you could always revive the traditional Easter Monday egg-rolling contest – all you need is one brightly coloured hard-boiled egg per person and a grassy bank to roll them down!

## PREPARING AND BLOWING THE EGGS

Any kind of egg can be used. Hens' eggs are the cheapest and are easy to handle, but duck, quail and goose eggs would be an unusual alternative.

In order to use the eggs for a ring, you will have to blow out their contents. (If you just want to decorate your eggs and do not want to blow them out, boil them for up to half an hour. Remember to prick them first to prevent the shells from cracking.) Pierce the shell at the top and bottom with a darning needle, making two small holes. Hold the egg over a bowl and blow hard through the top hole – the contents will come out of the opposite end, leaving the egg intact.

## DYEING THE EGGS

Before dyeing or colouring the eggs, ensure that they are clean and free from grease. Special Easter egg dyes are available, but the selection of colours is very limited. Fabric dyes offer much more variety, or you could even make your own vegetable dyes (see below). Check all dyes for safety before you let children use them.

If you are using vegetable dyes, boil the substance in water until you achieve the required shade and then strain the liquid. A dash of vinegar added at this stage will make the colours more luminous. For darker colours, leave the eggs in the dye bath for over an hour; paler eggs will need a much shorter time. Remove them when you are satisfied with the colour and let them dry in the air.

ABOVE: *A selection of decorative techniques: from the top, felt-tip pen, dye and varnish, paint and batik.*
OPPOSITE: *Felt-tip pen decorated eggs, wired into a circle. 'The nest' is composed of pheasant and guinea fowl feathers that have been attached to a simple wire ring. For technique, see pages 122-125.*

When the eggs are dyed and dried, rub in a mixture of one part oil to one part vinegar to protect the shells and give them a rich lustre.

## DECORATING THE EGGS

*Scraping* You must use hard-boiled dyed eggs for this technique. Use a knife to 'scratch' away a design.

*Batik* Use a pin to draw a pattern in melted wax on the egg. After dyeing, the areas under the wax will retain their pale colour.

*Blocking* Dip small flowers in oil and stick them to the egg. Place in the toe of a nylon stocking and tie a knot in the end. After dyeing, the imprint of the flowers will remain.

*Sponging* Dab the egg with a sponge moistened with dye. Allow the surface to dry before repeating the process with another colour.

## VEGETABLE DYE SELECTION

You can create some wonderful dye colours from natural ingredients, most of which can be purchased from good health food stores. If you want to eat the eggs after you have decorated them, make sure that none of the dyes is toxic.

| | |
|---|---|
| BLACK | alder bark, pussy willow |
| BLUE | logwood, mallow |
| BROWN | alder bark, onion peel |
| GREEN | nettle roots and leaves, spinach, young alder bark |
| RED | beetroot juice, madder, onion peel and vinegar |
| YELLOW | alder bark, caraway seed, onion peel, saffron |

# FEATHER CIRCLES

ABOVE: *A simple wired ring of goose, gannet and
seagull feathers houses some painted goose eggs.
For technique, see pages 122-125.*
OPPOSITE: *Similarly, spectacular peacock feathers,
attached to a simple wire base, coupled with
'scratched' Polish eggs.*

*Birds make their nests in circles, for theirs is
the same religion as ours.*
BLACK ELK

The meaning of the circle, a natural form with symbolic importance, is nowhere more evocative than in the art of the American Indian. This magical shape is the pattern for many native American settlements, is echoed in the shape of the tepee and the warrior's headdress, adorns ritual objects and is used in ceremonial body painting. Even ritualistic dances follow a circular formation.

In the Hako ceremony of the Pawnee tribe, the priest would draw a circle on the earth with his toe. This circle represented a bird's nest and was drawn with the toe because the eagle – the symbol of the Great Spirit – uses its claws to build its nest. Significantly, this action also symbol-ized the gods creating a world for people to live in. The American Indians firmly believed that the ancient, magical powers lay not only in the circle, but also in its making. Like most ancient societies, the American Indians thought that they were at one with the world and the circle-drawing ceremony drew upon and emphasized this powerful belief.

In all early cultures nature was treated with reverence and awe. In Welsh folklore, for example, the Eagles of Snowdon were oracles of peace or war – if they cried incessantly they were said to be mourning an impending calamity.

Keep your eyes open on country walks, as you could well find many different kinds of feathers to use in a circle. Even common birds' feathers have ancient meanings and charms – the magpie and owl are symbols of evil, whereas the swallow is said to carry two precious stones inside its body, a red one to cure insanity and a black one for good luck.

# CRAFTED FLOWERS

Traditionally, most wreaths or circles are made from natural ingredients that come from and provide a bond with the earth. However, using the many varieties and types of fake flowers readily available today, you could bring this tradition up to date.

Displaying a ring made from everlasting silk, plastic or paper flowers is an optimistic life symbol and also a celebration of all that is new. In China and Japan, vibrant, bright circles made from artificial materials are a popular way of marking a celebration such as birth, marriage or the arrival of an important guest. Because of the unusual way in which they are treated, materials and textures are revealed in a new way, as well as reflecting all the delicate artistry and exquisite craftsmanship of the East.

You could exploit the beautiful pearly shades of small seashells to create a traditional Peruvian circle of unique 'flowers'. These flowers are made by sticking shells together, using a strong, bonding glue. Shells with holes can be strung together, using fine florists' wire, and then wound into a simple wire ring.

Making circles is not always a serious business: you could make a fake flower circle just for fun. New combinations are often the most exciting and help to keep this ancient tradition alive.

BELOW: *Silk flowers are attached to a wire wreath. For technique, see pages 122–125.*

OPPOSITE: *This elaborate wreath is made of many small shells.*

# SUMMER

*Ring-a-ring o'roses,*
*A pocket full of posies*

# HERBS AND SPICES

ABOVE: *A Mexican wreath of garlic cloves that have been plaited together.*
OPPOSITE: *You can thread medium-gauge wire through chillis to create a vibrant circle like the ones shown here.*

Today, we tend to think of herbs mainly as seasoning plants, but historically their medicinal, aromatic and symbolic uses were just as important as their culinary role. Throughout northern Europe, a herb ring hung by the door of a house or in the kitchen was a symbol of welcome and bounty. *Das Richfest*, the German festival in which new homes were crowned with wreaths of plaited flowers and herbs specially chosen for good luck, illustrates perfectly the significance of herbs in the home.

A wreath is the most traditional way of storing and displaying herbs. For your own wreath you could try choosing herbs purely for their culinary, aromatic and symbolic qualities.

Their associations, however, are often of equal importance. Herbs and spices collected while on holiday and hung in your home will provide a year-long memento of your trip, as well as evoking the tastes and smells of the holiday.

Pick fresh herbs in summer, just before flowering. (Evergreen herbs such as thyme should be given a chance to grow again before picking.) Leave the stems long so that you have plenty to work with – they can always be cut later. Tie them into individual bunches of each herb and then bind them together with wire to form a wreath. Shaping the herbs and spices into a circle and moulding them so that they all point in the same direction gives the wreath a sense of movement and symbolizes the progression of the seasons.

A herb wreath is useful as well as decorative – just pull off individual herbs as you need them and add new ones as they become available. They will eventually dry out and become a new store of dried herbs.

Dried flowers are often added to herbal wreaths to provide more colour, but herbs have such a variety of texture, shape and smell you may want to enjoy them just as they are.

# THE LANGUAGE OF HERBS

| | |
|---|---|
| ANGELICA | *inspiration* |
| | |
| BASIL | *good wishes* |
| BAY | *glory* |
| | |
| CHIVES | *usefulness* |
| CORIANDER | *hidden worth* |
| CUMIN | *fidelity* |
| | |
| FENNEL | *flattery* |
| | |
| HYSSOP | *cleanliness* |
| | |
| LEMON BALM | *sympathy* |
| MARJORAM | *blushes* |
| MINT | *eternal refreshment* |
| | |
| OREGANO | *substance* |
| | |
| PARSLEY | *festivity* |
| | |
| ROSEMARY | *remembrance* |
| RUE | *grace, clear vision* |
| | |
| SAGE | *wisdom, immortality* |
| SORREL | *affection* |
| SOUTHERNWOOD | *jesting* |
| | |
| TANSY | *hostile thoughts* |
| TARRAGON | *lasting interest* |
| THYME | *courage, strength* |

*To make a herb wreath you can use any number of different plants.*
*The wreath shown below and opposite includes thyme, sage and chillis.*

*Lay out the fresh herbs on your work surface and divide them into small*
*bunches of equal size. Pull some medium-gauge wire from the spool.*

*Hold the first bunch against the wire, leaving about 2in (5cm)*
*spare at the end. Bind the stems firmly.*

*Take the second bunch and hold so that it covers the stems of the*
*first. Bind again with the wire. Continue like this until you achieve*
*the desired circumference. Cut the wire from the spool.*

*Tie the ends of the wire together, ensuring that the final bunch is full*
*enough to cover the join. For great effect, a second circle can be*
*added by threading green chillis onto wire.*

*A bountiful herb wreath, overflowing with parsley, sage, rosemary, coriander, bay, dill, thyme, fennel and chives.* For technique, see page 42.

# AROMATIC WREATHS

ABOVE: *Herbs and flowers – including rosemary,
sage, thyme, heather and* Stachys lanata *– are
attached to a straw base and evoke the tastes and
smells of Greece. For technique, see pages 122-125.*

OPPOSITE: *This circle of bunches of lavender and
dried poppy seed-heads wound together
could be hung in a linen cupboard. For
technique see pages 122-125.*

Historically, wreaths have either had powerful symbolic meaning or been valued purely for their decorative qualities. But there is a third quality which is increasingly becoming important with modern wreaths – that of function.

As well as looking beautiful, many wreaths can enjoy a practical role in your home. Hung in a cupboard, a circle of lavender will give your linens a luxurious scent, while sandalwood and Nicotiana will keep the moths away from your stored clothes.

The moist atmosphere of kitchens and bathrooms will draw even the most delicate of scents out of floral and herbal wreaths. The lovely, fresh smell of mimosa, lemon-scented geranium leaves and lemon verbena will help to disguise cooking smells. In the bathroom, try hanging a circle of cinnamon sticks and fir cones stuck to a cardboard base. Alternatively, you could simply tie small bags of pot-pourri to an existing wreath with a selection of pretty ribbons.

A wreath of cedar twigs and bark, sandalwood shavings (see page 100, for making wreaths out of wood shavings), cedar cones and pine hung in the hall would carry the fresh smell of woodlands into your home.

There is not a room in the house that would not benefit from the aromatic qualities of these special wreaths – and even after the scents have faded, the aesthetic appeal continues to linger.

# WEDDING RINGS

ABOVE: *Traditional Greek headdresses, for blessing the bride and groom. They are decorated with orange blossom.*

OPPOSITE: *Jasmine, roses, lilac and freesias were bound to vine (bride's hoop) and wire (circlet) bases. For technique, see pages 122-125.*

*I*n every society, traditional wedding ceremonies are loaded with ancient symbols intended to bless the couple with good fortune and fertility and ward off evil.

The unbroken circle of the wedding ring has existed since the time of the Pharaohs; in every society it has signified fidelity and perpetual renewal. The lovers' knot, the wedding cake and the bride's hat or headdress in the West and the floral crown worn in many Eastern countries – all are perfect circles intended to bless the couple with peace and unity. In Crete, special wedding bread is formed into a circle, and in many cultures, guests encircle the bridal pair in a wedding dance intended to protect them and bring them happiness in their life together forever afterwards.

The true lovers' knot remains a popular motif for wedding cakes, dresses and hats. Bunches of knotted ribbons represent the bonds of marriage, and in the seventeenth century brides wore them lightly stitched to their dresses – young men would try to snatch them off as brides' favours. This tradition continues today in the practice of men wearing buttonholes, the most usual consisting of fern and carnation which, appropriately, symbolize sincerity and eternal love.

Flowers play a significant part at any wedding. The reception hall is decorated with them, bridesmaids often carry floral hoops and, as well as carrying her bouquet or posy, the bride frequently wears a circlet of flowers on her head.

Traditionally, the bride's headdress was both circlet and wreath. It represented not only virginity and fertility, but also mourning for the old life of the bride as she passed into her new, married state.

For your special wedding 'ring', you might also like to choose different flowers for their associations and meanings (see page 26).

# A TRAVELLER'S MEMENTO

The circle shape provides a wonderful opportunity to commemorate as well as to celebrate. Many wreaths are made to mark special holidays, such as Christmas, Easter and the Jewish Feast of the Tabernacle, but you could also make one to celebrate your own personal festivals – a holiday or special outing can provide the inspiration for a truly unique circle, recording the process of your journey and any chance discoveries you may make on the way.

The instinct and passion of the collector is revealed in the work of artists such as Marcel Duchamp and Karl Schwitters. They made imaginative use of all kinds of *objets trouvés* to make a comment on society. You can use the circle form to make your own comment – a special way of capturing the mood of the moment.

The circle shown here reflects the warm tones and atmosphere of India. Gathering all of the memorabilia together – in this case, plants, Indian cigarettes, coins, money, hotel stationery, photographs, torn labels, ticket stubs and beads – and forming them into a ring makes the souvenirs last and the circle itself becomes part of the memory.

A 'travelling round' can be inspired by any trip. To make a memento like this, cut a 12in (30cm) circle from stiff card and use a strong, bonding glue to attach your collection of assorted ephemera to the base.

# FISHERMEN'S RINGS

ABOVE: *A simply tied rope circle made by a lone transatlantic sailor.*
OPPOSITE: *Fishing paraphernalia tied to a dried grass base with fishing line creates an unusual circle.*

*T*oday's trawlerman in his modern boat is just as aware of the cycles of the seasons, the winds, rains and tides, as his great-grandfather ever was. He has an equal respect for the dangers of the sea and still adheres to ancient rituals to protect himself from its power.

Once at sea, certain objects are still sometimes referred to in code. This applies particularly to ropework and the knots sailors invent and tie when they are becalmed at sea for days on end. Two ropes are 'bent together', never 'knotted' and a knot is always 'opened', not 'untied'

In traditional burials at sea, it is not only the body that is cast over the

*When the wind is in the east,*
*It's neither good for man nor beast.*
*When the wind is in the north,*
*The skillful fisher goes not forth,*
*When the wind is in the south,*
*It blows the bait in the fish's mouth.*
*When the wind is in the west*
*Then 'tis at its very best.*

side. Wreaths are also thrown ceremonially into the water because it is thought that they carry the soul, like silent prayer, to its resting place.

Weaving rope into a circle and inventing knots of your own can be an absorbing pastime. Such a circle can evoke all the myths and rituals of the sea, as well as reflecting your own ideas and feelings. It does not have to be complicated – the circle of rope shown here makes a strong visual impact precisely because its inventor has kept it simple.

Those who fish for a hobby rather than for a living are also inclined to think that one particular type of fly or float will bring them good luck. A colourful circle made from a variety of flys, hooks and floats would make an attractive and useful present for any freshwater fanatic.

# SEASHORE CIRCLES

To the American Indians, the circle was a potent symbol; it was much used in their imagery and customs. Circles were magical and, if they were used in the correct way, they could conjure up spirits that brought rain, fertility and animals to hunt.

The Navaho tribe drew circles in the sand as part of a ritual intended to give power and protection to its members. In their eyes, it affirmed the tribe's position at the centre of the world and warned off enemies.

Although its pull is now more recreational than mythological, many of us enjoy time spent by the sea as a

*In this circle*
*O ye warriors*
*Lo, I tell you*
*Each his future.*
*All shall be*
*As I now reveal it*
*In this circle;*
*Hear ye!*
THE SONG OF THE SEER,
SUNG BY SHORT BULL, A DAKOTA SIOUX

BELOW AND OPPOSITE: *Shells and sea urchin shells are stuck to wooden bases as lasting keepsakes of a special holiday – an ideal project for tiny hands.*

way of reaffirming our connection with the powerful forces of nature. As with the holiday circle (see page 50), it also provides us with an opportunity to gather suitable materials for making a circle. If you want to display your pebbles and shells in this way, you will need a sturdy base on which to glue them. A wooden one – perhaps made out of driftwood – would be ideal. Using a jig-saw, cut a 12in (30cm) diameter circle. Attach your shells with a strong, bonding glue. Children are natural collectors, so this kind of circle is always extremely popular with them.

# SEWING CIRCLES

Textiles provide one of the most versatile media for making special circles. Any form of needlecraft can be adapted to create keepsakes that are both original and personal - from patchwork and needlepoint to appliqué and collage.

Let the fabric be your guide, drawing your inspiration from its pattern, scale, colour and texture. It is probably a good idea to start with a simple idea and pin things together first; you can add interesting details as you go along. Children might enjoy making a collage circle from felt, as it is easier for them to handle.

A precious patchwork quilt could be made from fabric circles – try getting all the members of your family to contribute their own designs sewn onto a square patch of fabric. Such a quilt is an interesting way to reflect family unity and individuality simultaneously and, who knows, it may eventually become a loved and treasured family heirloom.

The great variety of texture and colour you can achieve with needlepoint makes it an ideal way to create a stunning circle. You could use the tones of the circle shown (above) as your model, or look around you in the garden for inspiration.

The tiny dolls (right) were bought in Mexico and sewn together to form a circle, a common theme in Latin American culture. It would be a unique gift for new parents, as it reflects the whole, protective and nurturing symbol of the circle.

# PEARLY KINGS AND QUEENS

RIGHT: *A pin-cushion circle could send a special message to a friend.*

OPPOSITE: *A collection of mother-of-pearl buttons and buckles are sewn onto black velvet.*

Traditionally, London's Pearly Kings and Queens were coster-mongers, or street vendors of fruit and vegetables, their name drawn from the Middle English word 'coster', meaning cooking apple. Their unique dress dates from the 1880s, when a cargo of fashionable Japanese pearl buttons arrived in London. One coster sewed them around the bottom of his trousers, creating a fashion that was soon to include Tree of Life, star, sun, moon, bird, and flower designs, even ancient fertility symbols, among its popular motifs.

One of the most impressive fabric circles can be made by adapting techniques used in pearly costumes. Dark fabric (right) provides a wonder-ful contrast for the lustrous pearl buttons and buckles. Using dress-makers' chalk, draw out a rough design onto a 2ft (60cm) square piece of dark fabric. Use white cotton to attach the buttons and buckles onto the fabric. You could use the decorated fabric to make a spectacular cushion or, alternatively, a wall-hanging (If you decide to hang your design, place it behind glass to preserve it.)

Another Victorian tradition – pin-cushion patterns (above) – can be adapted with equal success. Velvet, silk or satin all provide good back-grounds. Create your design or mes-sage using dressmakers' pins – shad-ing can be achieved by varying the height of the pins.

# AUTUMN

*The wheel is come full circle*
KING LEAR
WILLIAM SHAKESPEARE

# DRIED FLOWERS

RIGHT: Pansies, pressed between the pages of a
telephone directory, were stuck to
a 9in (22cm) circle of stiff card
with strong bonding glue.

OPPOSITE: A straw base was used for this dried-
plant wreath of thistles, hydrangeas, lavender,
Helichrysum, artichokes, everlasting flowers,
Stachys lanata and doves' feathers. For
technique, see pages 122-125.

Dried flower circles are one of the most ancient forms of adornment; their form, use and decoration are suffused with meaning. Archaeologists found a dried flower wreath on the lid of a sarcophagus in the burial pyramid of King Sekemket of Egypt and, although the flowers were placed in the tomb more than 4,500 years ago, they retained their texture and shape. Though it may seem remarkable, poppy seeds found in the tomb were planted and grew successfully. Interestingly, the Egyptian word *ankh* means both 'life' and 'wreath', and the placing of the wreath in the tomb signifies eternal life.

Virtually any flower can be dried; try experimenting with the flowers you grow in your garden. Choose plants for their colour, texture and scent. Pick them when the plant is quite young and when the dew has dried, although not in the midday sun. Hydrangeas, however, should be picked when they are older, when the petals are crisp to the touch. Always pick the full length of the stem; they can be trimmed later.

If you are making a circle for a special occasion, you might like to refer to The Language of Flowers (see page 26) and Herbs (see page 40). You could also make a dried flower circle to remind you of a special time. For example, you could gather some favourite flowers and plants from a beloved garden before you move house to create a memento of the happy times you spent there.

## AIR DRYING

This is the easiest method of drying flowers. Tie them in bunches – use elastic bands for this, as they will remain tight as the stems dry and shrink – and hang them upside down in a cool, dark room. Flowers with larger heads can be supported by threading the stems through some chicken wire supported by a frame. The wire must be placed high enough to let the long stems dry freely.

Make sure that the bunches are not too tightly packed so that air can circulate freely around the seedheads and flowers. This is particularly important with leaves, as they hold their moisture and will rot if packed too closely together.

## DRYING WITH SILVER SAND

For very delicate flowers, silver sand should be used. This can be purchased from any good florist. Pansies, delphiniums, forget-me-nots, orchids, lilies and young roses all benefit from this method of drying. Characteristically, the flowers will shrink slightly and deepen in colour.

A shoe box is the ideal container for this job. Cover the bottom with a layer of silver sand, about 2in (5cm) deep, and carefully place the flowers

*A spectacular wire-based wreath filled with sand-dried spring and summer flowers including daffodils, roses, hydrangeas, gypsophila and chrysanthemums.*

in the box, either singly or in small groups – make sure that they all lie in the same direction otherwise some of them may disintegrate when you pour the sand off them at the end of the drying process.

Gently trickle the silver sand over the flowers, trying not to let them touch one another. They should be covered in a fine layer of sand, though the shape should still be recognizable. Store in a dry place for at least ten days. To re-use the sand, dry it out in a low oven.

ABOVE: *A selection of dried everlasting flowers were attached to a straw base. For technique, see pages 122-125.*

OPPOSITE: *Provence was the inspiration behind this straw-based wreath containing thistles, hydrangeas, sage, thyme, dried grapes, lichen, olive leaves and a snake's skin. For technique, see pages 122-125.*

# HARVEST CELEBRATION

*And the feast of harvest, the firstfruits of thy
labours, which thou hast sown in the field;
and the feast of ingathering, which is in the
end of the year when thou hast gathered in
thy labours out of the field . . . the firstfruits of
thy land thou shalt bring into the house of the
Lord thy God.*

EXODUS XXIII, VERSES 16-19

*L*egends from rural cultures the world over try to account for the cycle of growth, death and rebirth in the form of seed. So magical and awe-inspiring did this natural cycle seem to early settlers, that they made offerings to the gods of the sun and moon to ensure a good harvest. These gifts were offerings to the gods, or idols, from which we get the term corn 'dolly'.

Most countries attribute the cultivation of grain to one mythological character. In Egypt, King Osiris was said to have taught his people to cultivate wheat and barley by breaking up the land in the Nile Valley after the annual flood had receded enough to sow the seed and later to gather in the harvest.

In India, Indra (the thunder god who brought rain to the dried-up Punjab) was the corn spirit and the god of fertility. After his battle with drought demons, the rain came and the maturing rice harvest was fed. A special cake, made with the new grain,

*OPPOSITE: A spectacular testament to the art of the corn dolly maker, illustrating the complexity to which this craft can reach.*

was given to Indra as an offering, and to the fire god, Agni, who brought the seed to life. In India today, rice straw designs are used as talismans or charms and are often found hanging in the doorways of homes intended for newly-married couples.

China, Japan, Greece, Scandinavia and Britain all have similar legends. In pre-Christian days, the corn spirits were offered human sacrifices. Animals were later substituted and later still the gifts became food and drink made from the newly harvested grain.

Harvest is a time rich with ancient customs, but of these, perhaps the most important is that of cutting the last sheaf. Reaping the last handful of corn in the field was a ritual all shearers treated with honour, and sometimes even with fear. Customs vary from region to region – some

countryfolk threw their sickles at the last sheaf until there was nothing left of it; in pre-Christian times the cutter of the last sheaf was killed to give life back to the corn spirit; other traditions hold that the last sheaf holds an evil spirit and so they trample it into the ground.

Traditionally, harvesters believed that as the crop was gathered in, the deity retreated, finally taking refuge in the last sheaf cut. In many cultures, this sheaf is preserved, dressed and decorated, often in the form of a corn 'dolly' – the characteristic circular or spiral shape being a suitable representation of the corn spirit's life cycle and a good way of preserving the old seed for the coming year. In spring, this corn was taken to the fields so that the spirit could be transferred to the newly-sown seed.

Each region has its own corn dolly specialities, such as the Bat's Wing or Flat Foot Rustic in England or the German Zwilling, reminding us that this is a truly international art.

ABOVE: *Bunches of ears of corn are added to the basic five-straw plait with natural coloured thread.*

ABOVE RIGHT: *The plait can be bent into different shapes, but it must first be soaked.*

OPPOSITE: *Bunches of wheat, oats and barley were bound to a straw base. For technique, see pages 122-125.*

## BASIC PLAITING

Before beginning to make a dolly, it is worth finding out about the different types of straw. Wheat is best for the beginner, provided you choose a hollow-stemmed variety; oats are softer and darker; rye tends to be harder.

The top length of the stem should be used for plaiting – that is, the piece from the ear down to the bottom of the last leaf where it leaves the stem. Begin by cutting this part of the straw away from the stems, strip off any dead leaves and sort the straws into thick, medium or fine groups – use thicker straws for big dollies and fine straws for more delicate designs.

Soak the prepared straws in cold water for approximately 15 minutes to

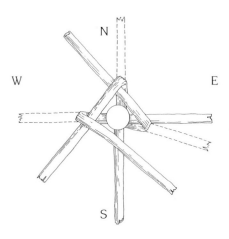

increase flexibility. Next, stand them upright to drain – they are now ready for you to use.

To make a small plaited ring you will need a selection of wheat stems

and a thin 16in (40cm) cane. Select five stems and tie the thin ends together around the cane using natural-coloured thread. Bend the straws away from the cane, at right angles to it, so you have 2 stems at North, and one straw at each of the other compass points. Take one of the straws at N and bend it over W. Next, bend W over S. Continue in this manner, building up the plait. When the straws become short, simply slot in the thin end of new straws-carry on in the same way.

Tidy the end of the plait with thread, and soak in water for 10 minutes so that you can bend the cane into a circle. You can either leave the circle plain or decorate it with suitable ornaments.

ABOVE: *Five-straw plaits make up these simple circles. In the foreground are small circles made by binding sheaves of corn to a straw base.*
RIGHT: *A selection of corn.*
OPPOSITE: *This traditional Swedish wreath was made from a giant plait of straw. The ends were bound together with a single stem.*

# GINGERBREAD AND CAKES

Gingerbread has many different myths explaining its origin. In England, the 'Johnny Boy', or 'London Bun', was originally a biscuit in the shape of a little boy who was said to have been captured and baked, but he came alive during cooking and escaped by unlocking the oven door. The Gingerbread Man is the most familiar pattern or shape, but you can choose any figures to make an edible decoration or a centrepiece that children will love.

### GINGERBREAD RECIPE
*8oz (225g/1 cup) plain flour*
*4oz (115g/1 stick) butter, cut into small chunks*
*4oz (115g/1 cup) soft brown sugar*
*1tbsp (15ml) molasses (black treacle)*
*1tbsp (15ml) golden syrup*
*1tsp (5ml) ground ginger*
*1 tsp (5ml) rum (optional)*
*1 egg white (optional)*

Sift the ginger and flour into a bowl. Rub in the butter and stir in the sugar. Add the molasses (treacle), syrup and rum and mix, using your hands, until the ingredients form a sticky dough. Wrap in aluminium foil and leave in a cool place overnight.

Preheat the oven to 350°F (180°C/gas mark 4). Prepare your template or pattern on paper and line a baking tray with non-stick silicone or grease-proof paper.

Unwrap the dough and roll it out on a lightly floured surface until it is about ⅛in (3mm) thick. Use pastry cutters or your paper pattern to help you cut out the shapes and arrange them in a circle on the baking tray. When you have transferred the dough to the tin, remove the paper.

Bake for 15 minutes or until golden. When cool, you could add icing or other cake decorations.

Another spectacular ring to make in the kitchen would be an iced cake. Using your favourite fruitcake recipe and a circular baking tray, create a 'base' for your icing designs. The following recipe makes 1lb (450g) of fondant icing.

### FONDANT ICING
*1lb (450g/4 cups) confectioners' sugar*
*1 egg white*
*2oz (60g/9tsp) sugar syrup (liquid glucose)*

Sift most of the sugar into a bowl and add the egg white and syrup (glucose). Mix with a wooden spoon; then knead the icing, adding the remaining sugar. To colour the icing, knead in drops of edible food colour.

You could mould your icing into simple flowers to make a seasonal gift. Alternatively, you could make a ring of tiny animals for a small child.

# BREAD CIRCLES

RIGHT: *Greek brioche, baked with a dyed egg in the centre.*

OPPOSITE: *Traditional Swedish bread – made for sharing.*

efore the introduction of money and coinage, the Egyptians used bread as a form of payment – perhaps the origin of our 'modern' slang for money, 'bread' or 'dough'? Breads of many different shapes and patterns are illustrated in Egyptian tomb paintings dating from as early as 1500BC. Some are shaped like fish and birds, and many appear to be coloured with earth pigments and decorated with seeds.

Although Eastern and Islamic cultures made differently shaped breads, ritual and festive breads tend to be more firmly associated with Europe. Germany, in particular, is famous for its decorative breads and during the baroque and rococo periods they became very elaborate – even to the extent of being used to portray important historical events, religious symbols and proverbs, and portraits of well-known people.

Historically, all societies celebrated harvest and spring. This frequently involved the offering of a sacrifice to the gods to ensure good harvests and continued prosperity. As civilization progressed, bread replaced game as the spring or harvest sacrifice and today, most cultures celebrate these festivals by baking a symbolic loaf.

Christian bakers, especially those in seafaring communities, often use the story of the loaves and fishes, or simply the symbol of a fish, for their festive loaves. Not only did this show respect for the sea and its hard-won bounty, but the fish represents rebirth and is one of the most powerful symbols of Christianity.

In arable areas, inspiration was more likely to come from the fields and crops or from birds, the symbols of air, so bakers made traditional wheatsheaves to celebrate an abundant harvest. These loaves still play a central role in the harvest thanksgiving, not least because they enable the baker to show off his talents.

Easter is the other festival commonly celebrated in many parts of the world by making breads and biscuits. In Poland, they make special biscuits in the shape of the farmer's wife feeding her geese; in Germany, the baker's Easter hare is a popular holiday gift and in Greece, a red egg symbolizing the Resurrection (see page 76) is baked inside brioche.

Many other ceremonies have their symbolic breads firmly embedded in the local culture and folklore. In Greece, specially decorated loaves weighing 40lb (18kg) or more are eaten during funerals as a ceremonial rite of passage. In Crete, wedding breads are seen as symbols of life and fertility and are given to the bride and groom. The Cretan breads are an integral part of the wedding ceremony itself and are baked in the bride's home with every member of the family lending a hand. These ornate breads are traditionally made in the form of a circle or wreath.

## TO MAKE HARVEST BREAD

Allow about four hours to make this loaf. Keep the dough moist and cool throughout and handle it with care.

HARVEST BREAD RECIPE
*3lb 2oz (1.4kg/6 cups) all-purpose flour (medium
strength bread flour)
1oz (25g/2tbsp) salt
1oz (25g/2tbsp) fat, preferably
lard, cut into small chunks
1oz (25g/2tbsp) milk powder
1 tsp (5g) dried yeast
1pt (750ml) cold water
2 eggs, beaten*

Sift the flour and salt into a large mixing bowl. Stir in the milk powder and the fat.

Dissolve the yeast in the water and pour it into the flour mixture. Knead the dough thoroughly until it forms a smooth, tight ball. Then, leave it to rest for about an hour, covering the top with a clean, damp cloth to ensure that a skin does not form.

When the dough is ready, divide it into three equal sections. On a lightly floured surface, roll each section in to a long sausage-shape, about 2in (5cm) in diameter. Plait the 'sausages' and form them into a circle on a greased baking tray. Where the two ends meet, pinch them into a bow shape and trim away the excess dough.

Glaze the whole circle with an egg wash to heighten the lovely golden colour of the finished loaf. Leave it to stand for 10 minutes and then brush with egg again. Allow the loaf to relax for 30 minutes at room temperature covered in a damp cloth. Keep it free from draughts and make sure that a skin does not form.

Bake in a moderate oven 400°F (200°C/gas mark 6) for one hour. Check occasionally to make sure that it is not burning – if it does seem to be browning too quickly, turn the oven down. When it has achieved its full shape and colour, remove from the oven and allow to cool.

RIGHT AND OPPOSITE: *Ornate bread rings are an integral part of Cretan wedding ceremonies.*

OVERLEAF: *A spectacular display of circular breads from around the world.*

# DRINKING WREATHS

RIGHT: *These lime twigs and leaves are wound onto a vine base. For technique, see pages 122-125.*

OPPOSITE: *Hop vines are twisted to form a self-supporting wreath. For technique, see pages 122-125.*

ince the dawn of history, Europe has been covered with vast forests. Travellers in Roman times could venture out for two months or more without leaving the entire Hercynian forest which stretched eastwards from the Rhine; in twelfth-century England, Londoners hunted wild boar and bulls in Hampstead. These immense acres of woodland were natural sanctuaries and became known as sacred groves throughout European culture.

The figure of the Green Man depicted in pub signs and in many medieval churches all over Great Britain is a strange composite of man and tree. The inclusion of this symbol in early Christian churches demons-

trates Man's reluctance to give up the faith born of instinct and superstition. The figure represents new life springing from death, endowing the tree spirit with creative power. A common sight at May Day festivities, the Green Man dressed in foliage and flowers would lead the parade. Like the cutting of the last sheaf and the plaiting of corn dollies, an ancient ritual was performed by hop pickers on the last day of the harvest. The foreman and a local woman were buried under hops in the basket used for collecting the crop. They were then 'resurrected', by being tipped out of the basket, to promote the healthy growth of next year's crop.

Traditionally, 'drinking circles' were

made from freshly picked and harvested crops. Hops and limes are often used in the preparation of such circles because of their distinctive aromas. The hops, in particular, remind us of the Green Man so frequently seen on British pub signs.

Like the Herb Ring (see pages 44-45), a lime – or camomile, or peppermint – circle is a practical and attractive addition to any kitchen, as the leaves can be used to make a refreshing and imaginative infusion.

This can be done by placing the leaves or flowers in a warmed teapot, adding boiling water and leaving the mixture to brew for 3 to 5 minutes. Strain and drink while the tea is fresh. Add honey as a sweetener if you wish.

# AUTUMN BERRIES

ABOVE LEFT AND RIGHT: *Assorted wild rosehips were wound into vine bases. For technique, see pages 122-125.*

OPPOSITE: *A cornucopia of gourds, berries, crab apples, medlars, rosehips, japonica and leaves on a vine base. For techniques, see pages 122-125.*

Rejuvenation, renewal and fertility are all celebrated at harvest time. A never-ending ring made from ripe, plump berries and gourds reflects the fecundity and richness of autumn and the eternal circle of the seasons. The autumn circle is both a celebration and the culmination of a year's work, representing as it does the fruits of labour and the seeds of future growth.

In the past, autumn berries had to be saved to provide seeds for the following year's crop. To ensure that they dry properly, it is essential that they are stored in a dry, open space where the air can circulate freely around the berries – thus the wreath shape is both supremely practical as well as decorative.

Although originally a pagan festival, harvest has always been a time for celebration and people still feel the need to give thanks by decorating churches with bread, fruit, flowers and vegetables, often arranged in the symbolic shape of a circle to reflect the cycle of the seasons.

Traditionally, wreaths were made from plants which formed a circle linking the maker and wearer to everlasting life. This wreath is a traditional harvest table decoration, plump and overfilled with quinces, medlars, gourds, rosehips, berries, crab-apples, holly, ash berries, baby tomatoes and asparagus. Gather in everything you can find before the frost sets in, bearing in mind how full your ring will be before you start making the frame (see pages 122-123).

The simple wreaths shown here symbolize the continuous renewal of life, a prayer of thanks for the newly-gathered crop and a blessing for the following year's harvest.

*A colourful assortment of berries, hips and haws were wound into a plaited vine base. For technique, see pages 122-125.*

# DRIED SEEDS AND LEAVES

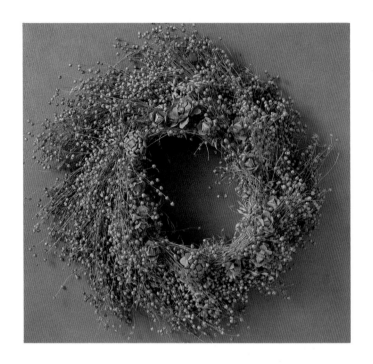

ABOVE LEFT AND RIGHT: *Dried flax and sandalwood flowers wound into a straw base, and a simple wreath of poppy heads also wired to a straw base. For technique, see pages 122-125.*

OPPOSITE: *This vine base is crammed with dried flax, poppy heads, honesty, Chinese lanterns, Mexican 'eggs of God' and speckled quails' eggs. For technique, see pages 122-125.*

*O*nce you have learned a few basic drying techniques (see below), you can explore the full range of colours, textures and shapes that certain grasses and plants acquire once dried. Draw your inspiration from rich autumn hedgerows, but remember, you do not have to stick too closely to nature. With this kind of arrangement, you can afford to be imaginative and bold.

You could start by experimenting with the plants you have in your garden or with the specimens you find when out on country walks.

## METHODS OF DRYING

Leaves and grasses dry well when they are air-dried flat. Leaves may shrivel but they will retain their colour and shape. Lay the leaves on an

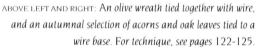

ABOVE LEFT AND RIGHT: *An olive wreath tied together with wire, and an autumnal selection of acorns and oak leaves tied to a wire base. For technique, see pages 122-125.*

OPPOSITE: *This eucalyptus wreath has a wire base and is displayed on a bed of lotus leaves. For technique, see pages 122-125.*

absorbent surface such as newspaper or cardboard and space the plants out so that their edges do not come into contact with one another.

The best method for preparing leaves and foliage for circle-making, however, is to preserve them with glycerine. This method maintains the texture, but the leaves will discolour quite dramatically.

Fill a large container with one-third glycerine and two-thirds boiling water and stir well. Prepare the plants by cutting the base of the stems at an angle so that they will take up the

mixture easily. Split and hammer any hardwood stems. Stand the plant stems in about 3-4in (7.5-10cm) of the mixture in the container. Store in a cool, dark place for about two weeks: check their progress after one week. They are ready when the colour has darkened and there are small drops of glycerine on the leaves.

Leaves which react favourably to this treatment are copper beech, eucalyptus, pine, oak, ivy, magnolia, choisya and aspidistra. This method is also effective for drying different types of heathers.

# SWEET CIRCLES

All Souls night, 31 October, has been associated with magic and witchcraft for centuries. In Britain and the United States, Hallowe'en celebrations are accompanied by certain games, charms and foods, all originating in ancient methods of warding off evil spirits.

An atmosphere of mystery still permeates the evening. Lanterns made from turnips or pumpkins, carried by children disguised with blackened faces, were originally an imitation of and protection from the lost souls said to walk the earth on this night. The bonfires and fireworks, such as Catherine Wheels, popular at this time of year have their origins in ancient, purifying fire festivals.

At Hallowe'en, an apple skin peeled in one unbroken strip and then thrown over one shoulder was supposed to reveal the initial of a girl's future husband; it was also thought that an apple eaten in front of the mirror while brushing your hair would encourage the reflection of a future spouse to appear. Bobbing and ducking for apples in a tub of water, attempting to eat an apple swinging from a beam or door lintel – these noisy, messy and amusing games are still played at this time of year.

When so many of these traditions involve apples, what could be a more appropriate centrepiece for a children's Hallowe'en party than a toffee-apple ring (opposite)?

As circles made from all forms of confectionery are both colourful and easy to make (simply attach sweets to a polystyrene base with toothpicks), they are a good way for children to contribute to party preparations. Charms and gifts are often included in pies eaten at Hallowe'en, so you could continue this tradition by attaching tiny going-home gifts to your circle ready for small guests to pick off as they leave – a popular idea at any time of year!

RIGHT: *Licorice and other sweets are knotted around wire to form this party centrepiece*

OPPOSITE: *A sticky circle made from toffee apples and bay leaves.*

# WINTER

*Here we go round the mulberry bush,*
*On a cold and frosty morning*

# THE ST LUCIA CROWN

RIGHT: *A wooden circle with candles forms the traditional St Lucia crown.*

OPPOSITE: *This circle makes an equally attractive table centrepiece.*

The Feast of St Lucia falls on 13 December and marks the beginning of the Christmas season in Scandinavian countries. Many centuries ago, St Lucy, the Christian saint traditionally associated with modesty and virtue, became connected with this pagan festival of light and fire to celebrate the winter solstice.

The Lucia procession is still a very common sight in Sweden. A young woman playing the part of the Lucia Queen or Bride is dressed in a white shift, symbolizing light, and a red sash, representing fire, along with a headdress of candles which combines the light and fire imagery. The procession is led by a figure dressed as St Stephen and the Lucia Queen follows, attended by her maids-of-honour, also bearing lighted candles, and masked trolls and demons who represent the darkness and evils of winter. The Queen visits every house and stable in the parish – it is considered a very bad omen if your house is deliberately or accidentally omitted!

In some areas, families have their own celebration, the Lucia Queen being played by the youngest girl in the household. She gets up before sunrise and dresses in the traditional costume, including a lighted crown. Then she takes cups of coffee to her family and, if they own any animals, she feeds them, before taking the place of honour at the breakfast table.

Like Queen of the May parades in England, the Feast of St Lucia is a joyful occasion. On this morning, bright lights shine out from homes and schools all over the Swedish countryside, reminding people that the darkness of winter will soon be over and that the celebrations of Christmas are on their way.

The young girl (above) is dressed as a traditional Lucia Queen. Her coronet, with its nine burning candles, is made from bilberry twigs. To be in keeping with the festival, it would be placed on her head before sunrise. If you are going to uphold this tradition, you had better supervise the proceedings very closely! Using non-drip candles is essential in order to avoid accidents with hot wax.

# SALT-DOUGH

RIGHT: A *glazed salt-dough circle depicting Noah's Ark and pairs of animals.*

OPPOSITE: A *salt-dough circle of theatrical masks is painted in vibrant colours.*

*S*alt- or sour-dough has been used by many cultures worldwide to make decorative objects, notably those in Ecuador and Mexico. Ecuadorian bread dolls are highly ornate representations of everyday life and depict peasants, shepherds and local animals. In Mexico, the most delicate jewellery is made from dough. It was the Mexicans who discovered how to preserve these artefacts by making a dough they called 'bread glue'.

The creative possibilities of this versatile substance are almost limitless. Salt-dough making is definitely an activity to share – and it is an ideal medium for small hands. It costs very little to make, so children can be given a free rein – a favourite salt-dough wreath is made from brightly painted pairs of animals circling in 'Noah's Ark' formation.

The basic salt-dough recipe consists of flour, salt and water, mixed and kneaded, then shaped, baked, decorated and sealed.

SALT-DOUGH RECIPE
*2lb (900g/4 cups) all-purpose (plain) flour*
*8oz (225g/1 cup) salt*
*1pt (450ml) water*

Combine the flour and salt. Add the water and stir with a spoon until the ingredients form a ball. Knead the dough until it has a smooth, 'satiny' texture. If necessary, add more water or flour until you achieve the right consistency.

Mixed dough dries out quickly when exposed to air, so seal the dough in a plastic bag and take out only what you need as you work.

When you have made your circle, brush it with an egg wash if you want

a glossy finish and place it on a baking sheet covered with non-stick silicone or greaseproof paper. Bake in a cool oven – 275°F (135°C/gas mark 1) – 325°F (160°C/gas mark 3) – until thoroughly dry and hard. You should allow half an hour's cooking time per ¼in (0.5cm) thickness. The higher the temperature, the browner the dough will become, so if you want a pale circle, bake at a lower temperature.

Thin and thick parts of the circle will brown at different rates so, to prevent unevenness of colour, cover the browned areas with aluminium foil. If bubbles appear, prick them with a pin and place a heavy object on top to keep it flat. Do this only when the crust is really hard, or you will dent the surface.

When the circle is cooked, remove from the oven and cool on a wire rack before decorating and/or sealing.

# SWEDISH CARPENTERS' CIRCLES

ABOVE: *Leaves on a vine base complement delicate flowers made from wood shavings.*

OPPOSITE: *This simple wooden circle is made with nails, tacks and hooks.*

$\mathcal{T}$raditionally, people have made circles and garlands from materials that were readily available to them – this accounts for the enormous national and regional diversity found in what is an essentially simple art. In Sweden, where timber has always been plentiful, it is not surprising that a traditional circle could be made from the small pieces of wood and bark left over from larger projects.

These inspirational Swedish wreaths, traditionally made by railway workers during their lunch-break from pieces of scrap wood, demonstrate that by using the materials around us,

the things we use each day, we can create something unique.

The circle provides a perfect way of expressing the theme of work. For example, a thoughtful gift for a carpenter could be made from a circular wooden base onto which you could attach the tools of the trade. Or use nails to create a message or an attractive motif.

Another suitable base for this kind of project can be made from twisted vines covered with a layer of leaves. Flower shapes made from folded wood shavings could be attached to the base with wire.

# CIRCLES FROM PAPER

ABOVE: *A simple paper or card cut-out stencil used with spray paints can create a charmingly colourful effect.*
OPPOSITE: *Gold adds the final touch to this papier mâché circle.*

𝒫aper and papier mâché have been used to make beautiful and useful objects for many centuries; indeed there are examples of Chinese papier mâché war helmets dating from as early as c.AD200. The appeal of papier mâché lay in the fact that it was strong, inexpensive and could be treated in a wide variety of ways – painting, inlaying, gilding and varnishing, to name but a few.

The simple materials required for this papier mâché technique have made it a popular folk art, especially in Eastern Europe and South America. The circle shown opposite is inspired by both of these cultures.

## TO MAKE PAPIER MÂCHÉ

For your papier mâché model you will need modelling dough, mould-makers' soap, newspaper, a large bowl, wallpaper paste and some acrylic paints. Prepare a template for the model you want to make before you start mixing the papier mâché.

Each part of your object should be moulded in modelling dough first.

ABOVE: *Cut and 'pricked' paper circle.*
OPPOSITE: *Traditional cut-paper Christening circle in a frame.*

Cover the model with a layer of mould-makers' soap first, as this will make the paper easier to remove.

Prepare the paste and tear six layers of newspaper into 2in (5cm) squares. Smear the paste evenly on both sides of the newspaper with your hands and then tear into strips ¼in (0.5cm) wide. Apply the strips to your model – taking care to smooth out any air bubbles – until it is covered. Repeat this process 5 more times.

Allow the model to dry overnight. You can now paint the model with your own design. If you use acrylic paint, you will be able to complete the decorating stage in one day. To make the circle shown, you may need to use several small moulds to create models that must be glued together.

## OTHER PAPER CIRCLES

Although stencils have hardly ever been as popular as they are today, they have been used as a form of decoration for hundreds of years: from the American Shakers to rural Scandinavia and India, stencils have adorned walls, furniture and trinkets. They require little paint and are a fast, inexpensive and fun way to brighten up your surroundings. And remember – the simplest stencils are sometimes the most effective.

Buy pre-cut stencils if you wish, but it is very simple to make your own. Use brown paper or an acetate sheet to draw out your pattern and then cut around the marked shapes using a sharp craft knife. After you have

attached the acetate sheet to the surface you wish to decorate (use masking tape for this), you are ready to start. You can use almost any kind of paint for this – aerosol spray paint is easy to use and quick to dry.

The stencil shown on page 102 forms a delightful circle which, though it may not have the lovely scent of a flower wreath, is everlasting in the truest sense of the word.

Victorian cut-paper decorations are also a source of inspiration in paper-circle making. Shown here (above and opposite) are particularly elaborate examples. They were made, first by folding and cutting the paper, and then by pricking with dressmakers' pins. The circle shown opposite was finished with paint.

# GOLD LAURELS

Perhaps the most evocative Greek image is that of the laurel wreath, dedicated to Apollo, god of the sun and of creativity. The Romans adopted the wreath to decorate their generals and soldiers – the highest honour was a circle of oak leaves, signifying bravery and patriotism. Eventually, along with the rise in power and prosperity of the Roman Empire, leaf circles were replaced with gold ones and they became the adornment of emperors.

This symbol has endured throughout history. Napoleon chose to be crowned with a circle of gold laurel leaves and many of the English crowns were originally wreaths. Across the world, many forms of military decoration are still based around this same motif.

Even in modern times, wreaths or circles are still used as a part of ceremonial life in Greece. At weddings, bride, groom and all the guests sometimes still wear this form of headdress (see page 48) – the flowers and design being chosen to represent good luck and fertility.

This stunning wreath (opposite) is made from a special form of gold foil available from good art supply stores. After you have cut the correct number of leaves, perhaps using real laurel or oak leaves as your guide, you should score the veins into the surface – a nail is ideal for this. It is a good idea to score the leaves on top of an old telephone directory to protect the work surface. Cut a piece of strong wire to the desired circumference and, starting from the middle, carefully wrap the leaves around the wire (using fine florists' wire), taking care not to leave any of it showing. The leaves should all point in the same direction. When you have covered one half of the wire, repeat the same process on the other half, this time pointing the leaves in the opposite direction. Curve the covered wire into the desired shape.

# REMEMBRANCE WREATHS

ABOVE: *A traditional French ceramic wreath for laying on the grave – an everlasting tribute.*

OPPOSITE: *A selection of evergreen leaves were attached to a moss base. For technique, see pages 122-125.*

*D*eath, because it is often so mysterious and indiscriminate, has always been surrounded with rites and customs designed to ease the departed soul on its way to heaven and to protect those left behind from evil spirits.

In rural English areas, before mourners set out to accompany a coffin to its burial place, it was traditional for them to be given rosemary and evergreen sprigs, symbolizing remembrance and everlasting life. These were then thrown into the grave as a promise to the dead that they would not be forgotten by the living.

In Victorian times, when the mortality rate was so high (particularly for children), mourning took on many new symbols. Whereas for adults, black or purple were the standard colours of mourning, for a young person the colour was white. Children's coffins were often white and snowy kid gloves were often pinned to the funeral wreath of a young girl with a virtuous reputation. Called the Maiden's Garland, this wreath was then displayed in the church.

Societies have always honoured their war dead, as we still do today. In England, the third Sunday in November, Remembrance Sunday, is traditionally the day on which respect is paid to the soldiers who fell in the two World Wars. In every village and town, the war memorial is draped with wreaths of poppies – as these were the flowers that grew in the fields where many of the men fell – and evergreen, the ancient symbol of honour and eternal life.

# THANKSGIVING

ABOVE: *Kumquats and bay leaves threaded on strong wire.*
OPPOSITE: *Evergreens and berries are wound together. For technique, see pages 122-125.*

In the United States, Thanksgiving falls on the fourth Thursday in November. For many it is a family celebration, the highlight of which is a special dinner. Usually the meal centres around a magnificent roast turkey, accompanied by bread or sausage stuffing, cranberry sauce, sweet potatoes, creamed onions, cornbread followed by pumpkin pie and all washed down with hot cider punch. Although this may be far removed from the celebratory meals of the Founding Fathers, modern Americans take this opportunity to give thanks, not just for an abundant harvest, but for the wealth of opportunity and freedom that the country has represented to many people.

Traditionally, Thanksgiving is also the day on which Christmas wreaths are first hung on the front door or above the fireplace. These are usually made from evergreens – good ones to use would be holly, laurel, mistletoe, balsam fir and scotch pine. The fir wreaths have the advantage of exuding a wonderful, fresh odour, especially if they are to be hung on a chimney wall where the heat of the fire will intensify the smell.

The wonderful variety of shade, texture and shape found in evergreen plants is enough to make a stunning wreath. If you want to decorate it, however, good trimmings are red berries such as cranberries, wild red rosehips and bittersweet.

Traditional Thanksgiving wreaths are among the most stylish circles you can make, and they are also among the most simple. For a wall-hung wreath, it is best to use a wire or vine base (see pages 122-5). If you are intending to use your wreath as a table centre, a polystyrene base bought from a florist has the advantage of being able to take small candles. Alternatively, you could use Oasis or a moss base with evergreens to create an effective table centre for a family celebration.

ABOVE: *Berries threaded into a moss base. For technique, see pages 122-125.*　　　OPPOSITE: *Cranberries pinned to a 10in (25cm) diameter polystyrene base.*

# APPLE ROUNDS

ABOVE: *A circle of shiny apples in snow.*
ABOVE RIGHT: *A dried apple ring.*

OPPOSITE: *Apples threaded onto wire can be used with an evergreen wreath.*

*L*ovely red apples are plentiful at this time of year on both sides of the Atlantic. For a dried apple ring, Red Delicious apples are often used because their skin is one of the deepest in colour and it retains it even after drying. You could experiment with apples grown locally.

To make a dried apple ring you need:
13-15 *large red apples*
*1pt (450ml/2 cups) reconstituted lemon juice*
*1oz (45g/3tbsp) salt*
*1fl oz (45ml/3tbsp) citric acid*
*large wire cake rack*
*12in (30cm) double wire wreath*
*florists' wire*
*hot glue gun*

Pre-heat your oven on its lowest setting. Mix the lemon juice, salt and citric acid in a large bowl. Then cut the apples cross-wise into about ¼in (5mm) slices, either by hand or with a food dicer, saving only those pieces which have the star-shaped pattern formed by the seeds. Soak the apples in the lemon mixture for approximately five minutes.

Drain the apples on paper towels and then lay them on the wire cake racks. Place them in the pre-heated oven and leave them to dry out for six to eight hours. By this stage, they should be very leathery and slices cut in a food dicer will probably have curled slightly at the edges.

If you are going to hang your wreath, at this stage form a hanging loop on the back of the wire wreath using florists' wire.

Divide the slices into two piles – one pile for the most beautiful pieces, which you will use for the front of the wreath, and the other for the less-than-perfect ones you can use for the back. Using the hot glue gun, lay the slices around the wreath, overlapping them as you go. Once dry, gently turn the wreath over and repeat the process on the other side.

Bows, cinnamon sticks, aniseed stars and other spices can be added to this wreath, but it looks beautiful just as it is.

114

# CHRISTMAS

ABOVE: *This circle is made of glass, but you could make a similar decoration from ice.*

OPPOSITE: *A generous wire-based wreath including evergreens, crab apples, fir cones and decorative 'nests'. For technique, see pages 122-125.*

*B*ringing greenery indoors to decorate homes and other buildings at the winter solstice is a very old custom. One of the earliest examples known was the practice of wealthy men giving garlands of laurel and bay leaves to their poorer neighbours during the Roman Saturnalia. At their New Year feast, there was another exchange of gifts, or *strenae*, this time between relatives and friends. Traditionally, these were simple branches of greenery, thought to bring good luck because they were gathered in the groves of the goddess Strenia.

The true origin of this winter custom is probably as old as time – for evergreens flourish when all other plant life is dead, and so they have always been seen as magical symbols of undying life. The most popular seasonal decorations, past and present, are holly, ivy and mistletoe. These are very powerful life symbols because they bear fruit in winter and holly and mistletoe in particular have their own mythology wherever Christmas is celebrated.

Prickly holly with red berries is supposed to be lucky for men, whereas the smooth, variegated female holly plant is said to bring luck to women. Holly wreaths are not only symbols of good fortune; they also represent the continuous cycle of life and are still laid on family graves in England at Christmas time. They are a sign of 'undying', of returning to the earth and of hope. In the United States, similar rings are hung on front doors to celebrate Thanksgiving and Christmas, anticipate the return of Spring and confer a special blessing on the house.

In the past, it was considered bad luck to bring the Christmas greenery in before 24 December, and we still observe the tradition today of leaving decorations up until the twelfth night. The disposal of greenery has many customs – the belief is still held by many that no branch of holly which

116

has remained green should ever be burnt or misfortune will come to the family. On the Welsh border in Britain, a bowl of snowdrops is brought in after the holly, ivy and mistletoe have gone. This is said to drive out evil in preparation for the beginning of the spring season.

Perhaps the most 'romantic' symbol of midwinter is the sprig of mistletoe, which is supposed to be a fertility charm, a protector from evil and a remedy for numerous illnesses. It is the 'Golden Bough' of legends, which lit Aeneas' way during his descent into the Underworld and ensured his passage across the infer-

BELOW: *A vine-based evergreen wreath including variegated ivy, mistletoe, sage, bay and variegated holly. For technique, see pages 122-125.*

nal river Styx. It is a sacred plant believed to hold the life of its host tree and if it grows on an oak it holds – according to Druid myth – the seminal fluid of the oak tree god in its pearly berries. White-robed Druids would ceremoniously cut the mistletoe with a golden sickle on the sixth day of the moon and then fasten sprigs above their doorways to protect them from evil. It is as a result of these pagan rites that many Christians will not have mistletoe inside their churches: it may hang in the porch but *never* in the body of the church.

This magical bough can also reveal hidden treasure. Known as 'fern-seed'

ABOVE: *Different types of variegated ivy were wound into a vine base. Non-drip candles were added to create a warming centrepiece.*
OPPOSITE: *A post-Christmas table decoration, with an abundance of camellias.*

in popular mythology it blooms like gold or fire on Midsummer's Eve. In Russia, if you caught sight of this bloom on fire at midnight on Midsummer's Eve and threw it up in the air it would fall like a star on the exact spot where treasure was hidden.

A story told in Germany relates how a hunter shot at the sun on Midsummer's Day at noon. Three drops of blood fell which became fern-seed in his hand. Hence, the golden fire, as the seeds emanated from the sun. This glowing mistletoe was always gathered twice a year, on Midsummer's Eve and at Midwinter. To the Romans, 25 December was *Dies Natalis Invicti Solis* (birthday of the unconquered sun) and throughout the northern pagan world fires were lit during the winter solstice to welcome back the sun. Glowing candles, a warm fire and lighting the brandy on the pudding are still symbols of Christmas today.

It is likely that the custom of having a Christmas tree in the house developed from the practice of decorating homes with evergreens, although one legend in Victorian times, when such a tree became popular in Britain, ascribed it to Martin Luther. He was inspired by the winter stars shining through the branches during a walk in the forest and thought that a candlelit tree at home would remind his family of the glittering heavens.

In England, the Christmas tree replaced the traditional kissing-bough. This was a garland or circle of greenery shaped in a double hoop, decorated with candles, coloured paper, red apples and all kinds of ornaments, with a bunch of mistletoe suspended from the centre. The candles were ceremoniously lit for the first time on Christmas Eve and every night thereafter for twelve days. It hung from the middle of the ceiling in the main living room and was the centre of all family activities.

Making your own Christmas circles to hang on the door, on the wall or for a table decoration can still be the centre of family activities – encourage everyone to contribute and to collect the ingredients when they go for a walk or simply a forage in the garden.

aking circles or wreaths is a very simple skill to acquire. The basic tools required are a pair of strong scissors to cut the materials and fine wire or string to bind them to the base. Pliers and/or secateurs are also useful for cutting flowers and vines. For circles such as the Seashore Circles (see pages 54-5) or the Traveller's Memento (see pages 50-1), you will need specific equipment such as glue and floral picks or pins.

You will probably have some of the materials required in your home already, and the rest can be obtained from your local florist or hardware store. Most of the circles and wreaths featured in this book are built upon one of the simple bases outlined in this section. After you have mastered the basics, you can begin to create your own circles using almost any material that inspires you.

### MAKING A BASE

Usually, bases are made from vines, moss, wire or straw. They are available commercially, but you might like to try making them yourself. Other materials include wood, used for the base of the Swedish Carpenters' Circles (see pages 100-1), and stiff card which forms the base of the Traveller's Memento (see pages 50-1).

It is vital that you choose the type and size of your base according to the materials you are going to use to

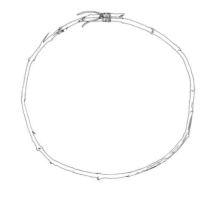

*The construction of a vine base.*

decorate it. At this stage, you should think about the way in which it is going to be used – whether it is going to be laid flat on a table or hung on the wall. If you are going to make a circle packed full of berries and gourds (see page 85), you will need to make a large base to take the weight of the decoration and to give it a sense of balance and proportion. This particular ring would be used to decorate a table rather than a wall.

The next consideration is how to fix the materials to the base. If you intend to use glue, you should ensure that the surface of the base is clean and dry. Check that the glue is compatible with both the type of base and the form of decoration you want to use.

Last, but not least, consider the look of the base itself. Will it be part of the look of the circle, or fully covered? For example, a partly exposed vine base will look very attractive in floral and herb circles, but chicken wire does not have the same aesthetic appeal.

### VINE

All you need for this frame is fine florists' wire, a pair of pliers and fresh vine stems. Wisteria and honeysuckle are the most usual vines used for circles, but you could experiment with any other suitable garden creeper.

If the vines used are not fresh, begin by soaking them to make them pliable. Cut the stems into lengths approximately 4ft 8in (1.40m) long. (The lengths depend on the circumference of your circle and do not have to be precise.) Make a circle with one length of vine and secure it with some wire. Attach the second length close to the join and twist it around the circle. Continue doing this with each stem of vine, catching any shorter lengths as you go, until you have the volume you require. Cut the wire away and you will find the vines will hold themselves in place.

● Use this type of base to make the wreaths featured on pages 24-5, 27, 49, 82, 83, 84, 85, 86-7, 89, 100, 111 and 120.

### SPHAGNUM MOSS

A wire base is the easiest to use with delicate moss fibres. You can either buy one from a florist, or try making one yourself. A simple circle can be made by pulling the wire of a coat hanger into the desired shape. For wall decorations you could leave the hook in place.

If you are making the base from scratch, cut strong, medium-gauge wire to the length of your circle's circumference plus about 4in (10cm). Bend back roughly 2in (5cm) at both ends of the wire. Attach fine florists' wire to the loop made by the bent-back wire of the base.

You can now start covering the frame. Begin by pressing a clump of

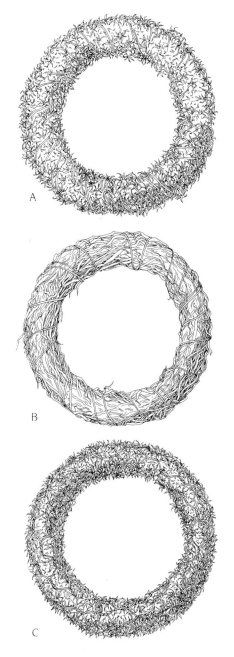

A *moss*; B *straw*; C *moss and chicken wire.*

moss onto the wire base and secure it firmly by wrapping the fine florists' wire around it several times. Repeat this each time you add a fresh handful of moss. Make sure that there is a slight overlap between the clumps and try to maintain a thickness of about 2in (5cm). When the frame is fully covered, join the ends by hooking the two loops of thick wire together. Cover the join with an overlapping handful of moss, secure it, and then tie the end of the fine wire to its starting point and trim it close to the knot.

If you are making a dried flower ring, allow the moss to dry completely in a cool place before you use it.

Chicken wire is also a suitable base for moss. You will need about a 1ft (30cm) width of chicken wire cut to the required circumference of your circle. Lay the chicken wire flat on your work surface and arrange the moss along one edge in an even layer. Roll the chicken wire tightly over the moss, tucking in the moss and any protruding wires as you go. The finished tube should be about 1½in (4cm) in circumference.

When you have finished, curve the tube around to form a circle, butting the two ends. Cut a length of florists' wire, attach it to one end leaving 2in (5cm) for fastening off and bind the ends of your circle together. Then tie the two 'spare' ends of wire together and conceal them in the base. Again, remember to let the moss dry if you are going to use dried flowers.

• Use a moss base in order to make the wreaths featured on pages 109 and 112.

### STRAW

Straw bases are widely available through craft shops and florists. They can be used with glue guns (also available from florists) and wire.

• Use a straw base to make the wreaths featured on pages 38, 46, 63, 66, 67, 71 and 88.

### WIRE

Simple wire rings are available commercially, but you might consider making one yourself. You will need a 3ft (90cm) length of medium-gauge wire. Bend the ends of the wire into hooks and join them up to form a circle. To make a bride's hoop, you will need approximately 4ft (120cm) of thick-gauge wire.

• Use a wire base to make the wreaths featured on pages 18, 31, 32-3, 34, 47, 49, 64-5, 92, 115 and 117.

### WIRING

Wiring is an important technique for reinforcing and strengthening flowers and plants with weak or fragile stems which might otherwise break when manipulated. Wiring can be done before or after drying, but it is advisable to wire delicate flowers when they are still fresh. Wire can also be used to bind together clusters of corn, dried grasses, feathers, flowers, herbs or other plants for easier application onto the wreath.

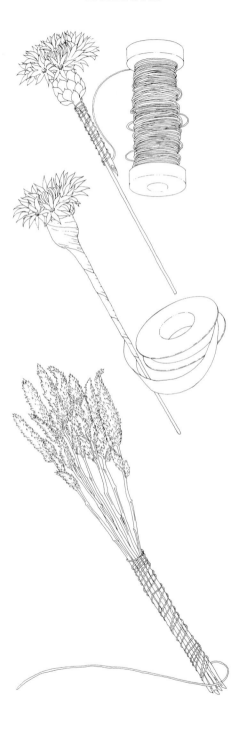

*Wiring single stems and clusters.*

### STRENGTHENING PLANTS

You will need a wire cutter or florists' scissors, medium-gauge stub wire, a spool of fine florists' wire and florists' tape (either brown or green depending on the predominant colours in your wreath).

For wiring flowers with weak, fragile or short stems, cut the stem to approximately 2in (5cm). Place the stub wire (the length you want the finished stem to be) against the stem so that it is touching the base of the flowerhead. Pull some fine wire from the spool and line a length along the stem. Hold the stem, stub wire and the length of fine wire in one hand and begin wrapping the wire attached to the spool tightly around the stem and the stub wire with the other hand. Continue to the end of the stem. Cut the fine wire and fold over the end. To disguise the wire you will need to wrap the stem with florists' tape. Hold the wired flower upside down and place the end of some florists' tape behind the stem at the base of the flowerhead at a 45° angle. Fold in the end of the tape and then twist it around the stub wire, fine wire and stem, keeping the tape taut so that it spirals up and just overlaps itself. Continue to the end of the stub wire.

Alternatively, you can completely replace the flower stem with wire. This technique is particularly appropriate for helichrysums. Insert a length through the base of the flowerhead and up through the flower centre. Bend the top of the wire into a hook and carefully pull it towards the stem so that the hook is firmly embedded in the flowerhead. Fold the hook so that it is securely fastened. Wrap the 'stem' with fine wire and florists' tape as described above.

### WIRING CLUSTERS

Wiring clusters of flowers, corn, feathers or plant material together will increase your design options and save time when you assemble your wreath. Clump material with similar 'stem' lengths together. Wire them together tightly and securely with fine florists' wire, to make a sturdy stem. Wrap the wired stems with florists' tape unless they are to be inserted into a moss base that will conceal the wire.

### WIRING A WREATH

A simple way to make a fresh flower or herb wreath is to use wire only. You will need medium-gauge wire and a good quantity of plant clusters (see above).

Pull a length of wire from the spool and, leaving a 2in (5cm) end, wrap firmly around a cluster. Wrap another cluster to the first, ensuring that the stem of the first cluster is well concealed. Continue adding one cluster after another until you have a length of approximately 2ft (60cm). Cut the wire from the spool, shape into a circle and wire the ends together with fine florists' wire.

Use this technique to make the wreaths featured on pages 16 and 42-5.

### ADDING TO A BASE

Clusters and single flowers with wired stems can be attached directly to a vine or thick wire base by inserting the wired stems and wrapping them around the base. Metal bases can be

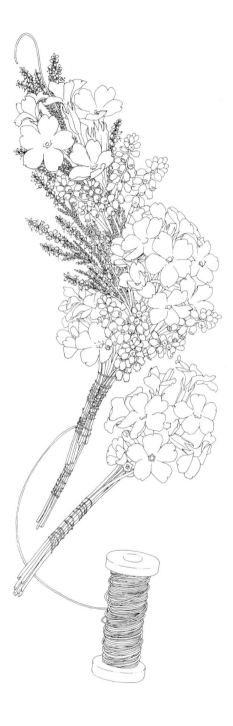

*Wiring clusters into a wreath.*

unattractive, so cover them completely with plant material, flowers or moss. Clusters, flowers without wired stems or single feathers should be placed on the base in the desired position and attached with fine florists' wire. Remember to overlap as much as possible to give a generous, full wreath.

### ATTACHING DRIED MATERIALS

The easiest way to attach clusters of dried material to a straw base is with floral picks, available at a crafts shop or a florist. Clusters can also be wired directly onto a vine base.

### ATTACHING ARTIFICIAL FLOWERS

Floral picks or U-shaped pins can also be used to attach artificial flowers. Alternatively, a glue gun can be used with a suitable wreath base, such as one made of straw or wood.

### FRESH FLOWER TABLE WREATHS

A long-lasting fresh flower table wreath can be made using a chicken wire base filled with sphagnum moss which has been moistened with water. You will need to cut the stems of the flowers to a length of approximately 2in (5cm), depending on the size of the blooms. Insert the fresh material into the wreath base making sure that all stems are fully 'buried' in the moss. Alternatively, a circle of Oasis in a dish will provide a suitable base for fresh flowers. Keep the Oasis moist to prolong the life of the wreath.

## PRESERVING WREATHS

To prolong life, fresh flower wreaths should be placed in a cool location. Set the wreath on moist paper or cloth towels and mist with water.

A fresh flower wreath can be dried by hanging it in a warm and well-ventilated room such as a kitchen. Alternatively, you can use a desiccant. Silica gel is especially suitable for drying delicate flowers which may have been used in a wedding wreath. The best sources of silica gel are chemists or shops selling flower arranging equipment. The best weight and grade for drying wreaths is the finely ground white gel.

Put a thin 1in (2.5cm) layer of silica gel in an air-tight tin or plastic container. Lay the wreath gently on top, facing upwards. Pile the silica gel gently around the petals and leaves. Using a fine brush, carefully work the desiccant between the petals making sure every part is totally covered.

Check the wreath after 48 hours. Be careful of leaving the wreath in the silica gel for too long as the plant material may become brittle. When the wreath is dry, remove it from the silica gel.

A delicate dried wreath should not be placed on a door that is constantly opened and shut. A very hot and sunny location may also damage and fade the plant material on your wreath. To store dried wreaths, place loosely in paper bags in a dry, well ventilated location. (Plastic bags will cause condensation that may damage your wreath and may cause mould and mildew to form.)

# INDEX

# ACKNOWLEDGEMENTS

The author and publisher would like to thank the following people for their contributions: Fiona Barnett, pages 17, 49, 109, 118-9; Peter Atkinson (Springfield Nurseries), page 19; Frank Mulville, page 52; Tessanna Hoare, pages 53, 92, 101; Elizabeth and Celia Juckes, page 56; Margaret Stanley, pages 15, 58; Polly Hope and Leonard Childs, page 59; Nora Albarda, pages 64-5; Ruth Wylie, pages 69-73; Jane Harborne, page 76; Celia Ceder, page 79, 96; Elsa Day, pages 78-81; Nicola Easton, page 75; Trim Hahn, pages 84, 110, 114; Jane Suthering, page 93; Caroline Bucknall, page 98; Jeff Hoare, page 99; Lyn Le Grice Stencil Designs Limited, page 102; Deborah Schneebeli-Morrell, pages 103, 105; Andrew Sterne, page 116.

The author and the publisher would also like to thank Geoffry and Dorothy Powell and Trim Hahn for allowing their homes to be photographed, and Neal Street East, the Conran Shop and Sante Fé for lending material for photography.

The author would like to thank Prue Bucknall, Anne Furniss, Polly Powell and Mary Evans for their help in the production of this book.

The publisher thanks the following photographers and organizations for their kind permission to reproduce the photographs in this book:

6 above left Science Photo Library; 6 above centre NASA/Science Photo Library; 6 above right Dr. Ann Smith/Science Photo Library; 6 centre left Michael Holford; 6 centre Syndication International/Aldus Archive (British Museum); 6 centre right Bridgeman Art Library; 6 below left Scala, Florence; 6 below centre Christian Sarramon; 6 below right Zefa Picture Library; 7 above left Dr. Jeremy Burgess/Science Photo Library; 7 above centre Zefa Picture Library; 7 above right Martin Dohrn/Science Photo Library; 7 centre British Library/Bridgeman Art Library; 7 centre right Robert Harding Picture Library; 7 below left Zefa Picture Library; 7 below centre Zefa Picture Library; 7 below right Zefa Picture Library; 22-3 Tania Midgley; 106 Zefa Picture Library.

The following photographs were specially taken for Conran Octopus:

Jan Baldwin: 3, 8, 14-5, 17, 19, 27, 30, 32-5, 38-9, 44-53, 55-59, 63, 66-69, 71, 72 above, 75-6, 79-81, 83, 85-91, 98-99, 101-105, 107, 118-9, 126.

Jacqui Hurst: 2, 10, 16, 18, 20 1, 22 inset, 24-5, 28-9, 36, 40-3, 60, 70, 72 below, 94, 93, 108-9, 116-7, 120-1.

David Phelps: 84, 110-115.

Courtesy of Elizabeth Iane Lloyd: 1, 31, 54, 62, 64-5, 73-4, 77-8, 82, 96-7, 96, 100.